"How does one become a Certified Public Accountant (CPA)?" I have been asked this question countless times throughout my career. While there are some excellent websites and other resources available, I have come to realize that there is no one single place to get answers. I have written this book to give the reader a concise yet informative roadmap to the steps it takes to become a CPA. It is designed to take the average reader approximately one hour to complete. Upon completion, you will not only understand the steps involved but also the benefits of entering this profession. I also throw in a little advice along the way regarding things that I wish someone had told me in college and the early stages of my career.

This is an amazing profession from which there are endless opportunities to grow both personally and professionally. I believe that it is underrated by both parents and students when looking into career paths. The combination of growth and earning potential far outweigh most other professional careers in the United States, not to mention job security. Most of these jobs remain intact during periods of economic downturn. Most accountants I know, including myself, are rarely ever looking for work but when we are, there are plenty of options from which to choose.

I hope you enjoy this book. I did my best to impart 30 years of knowledge and experience to you in just one hour. Why is this book designed to read in one hour? The answer is simple. So many books are never finished. I decided that the best way to reach aspiring accountants is to design the book in a format that would be read from cover to cover. Please don't hesitate to like my LinkedIn

https://www.linkedin.com/groups/13717660/ and/or
Facebook page
https://www.facebook.com/HowtobecomeaCPAin1Hour
"How to Become a CPA in 1 Hour" . If you have additional
questions about the accounting profession you can email me
at davidscottcpa@yahoo.com.

Contents

Chapter 1 - Why Should I Become a CPA?

When I started my more than 30 year journey through the various phases of becoming and working as an accountant, I had no idea the amazing places that it would take me personally, professionally and financially. I have traveled the country, eaten at great restaurants, met influential people all while making a reasonably good living for myself and my family. The accounting profession will open doors that you cannot imagine and create opportunities that few other jobs can. I have owned or currently own over a dozen businesses in the areas of healthcare, real estate, tax preparation franchises, horse racing, and accounting services. I have also had the privilege of being an adjunct college professor teaching a variety of accounting and business classes at multiple colleges.

While much of this book is dedicated to explaining the steps involved in becoming a CPA, it's essential to understand the benefits of entering this profession. Within this chapter, I have addressed what are typically the nine most common attributes that aspiring professionals are looking at when selecting a career path.

Money

The number one factor that drives most of us to work is the desire and need to support ourselves. Considering the diversity of the opportunities available, this is the most challenging of the nine attributes to breakdown. Most aspects of our daily lives involve accountants in the background, making sure that goods are available, services are performed, and structures are built and maintained.

Considering the education, expertise and experience required of accountants, they are some of the highest paid individuals in most organizations.

So, how much money is there to be made? Consider this. The four largest accounting firms in the United States, commonly referred to as the "Big Four", employ over 1 million people worldwide and generate a combined annual revenue in excess of 150 billion dollars. These firms are just the tip of the iceberg. Now consider the combined monies earned by firms of all sizes not to mention those accountants in private industry, not-for-profits and government. Besides, there are many ways for accountants to generate revenue. This includes, but are not limited to; auditing, taxes, various analyses, feasibility studies, fraud investigations, forensic accounting, risk and compliance, payroll, plus becoming senior accountants, controllers, chief financial officers or vice presidents of finance. Also, the academic world has a significant shortage of accountants with PhDs whose starting salary could be upwards of $125,000 annually, depending on industry and location. There are incredible opportunities for earning extra income through part-time teaching, serving on boards that compensate, preparing tax returns, consulting and general accounting services.

The United States Bureau of Labor Statistics reported a 2018 median annual pay nationwide for accountants of $70,500 annually as compared to $51,960 for all workers.[1] That being said, I feel the best source for detailed accounting salary information is the Accounting and Finance Salary Guide published by Robert Half. This company specializes

---

[1] "Bureau of Labor Statistics." https://www.bls.gov/. Accessed 18 Jan. 2020.

in employment services for various industries including accounting. Valuable information is abundant in this guide regarding trends within the industry. Additionally, it details average salary information in the areas of corporate accounting, public accounting, financial services, and healthcare. It also provides an easy to use guide with regards to convert the nationwide average salary into what you should expect in various cities throughout the United States. The guide outlines numerous benefits offered to accountants, as well as what to expect during the on-boarding period at a new job. This report is free. Go to https://www.roberthalf.com/salary-guide/accounting-and-finance and sign up for more information.

While you can earn an accounting degree without ever becoming a CPA, you will most certainly be leaving money on the table. That is why this book is focused on becoming a CPA. Approximately 50% of accountants will become certified and will earn a minimum of 10 - 15% more during their career and have greater job security than an accountant that is not a CPA. This is because CPA's are allowed to provide certain services that an accountant who does not hold a CPA license cannot, for example, signing financial statements. CPA's are considered among the most trusted professions in the business world. Additionally, most states don't allow anyone other than a CPA to become partners in CPA firms, a job with tremendous earning potential. This will be discussed in greater detail in Chapter 4.

Security

After money, the average person sees job security as the next most vital attribute to consider when deciding on a career. You will find that the older you get; the more crucial security will become to you. Studies show that most young people believe that they will have to work longer than the generations before them. This makes your choice of professions even more meaningful. In this age of ever increasing technological advances, we have seen the elimination of jobs, but we have also seen new industries created, as well as job transformation. The accounting profession has not only survived but continues to see growth and evolution. Over the years, accounting and tax programs have become more sophisticated. This has necessitated the creation of new jobs to use and monitor the systems. Economists widely agree that since the Great Depression in the 1930s, the United States has seen 13 distinct recessions. As history has proven to repeat itself, this would indicate that in all likelihood you will experience multiple economic slowdowns during your career. This is a consideration that is rarely thought about when choosing a career path. The cold hard reality is that these times can be devastating to an individual in many ways including the loss of assets they have spent a lifetime acquiring. This would include cars, homes, savings and businesses. For the most part, the accounting profession has been considered recession-proof regardless of economic conditions; it is virtually impossible for organizations, including government, to function without accountants. Recession or not, various companies, not for profits, and governmental units require audits and various tax returns filed.

In times of economic trouble, there will be an increase in the need for accountants, especially in the areas of tax and auditing. Companies and individuals will attempt to gain the maximum that they can from the current situation. Even local and state governments will increase their auditing staff during prolonged economic downturns in an attempt to recoup uncollected income and sales taxes. Additionally, there is usually a greater need for accounting instructors during these times as colleges see increased enrollment of people seeking to be retrained. Accounting is always one of the more attractive fields to these individuals because of the demand.

Staffing cutbacks within organizations are typically the result of adjustments to their budgets. Remember that accountants are heavily involved within the budgeting process and therefore have a greater ability to protect not only their own position but the jobs of their valued coworkers. Also, accountants are usually not as dispensable as other positions when budget cuts occur.

Job Mobility

Where do you want to live? This is a question that I often ask aspiring CPAs to make the point that there are jobs everywhere in the world for them. As we will discuss in detail later each state, as well as, the five United States territories are called Jurisdictions for licensing purposes. Therefore, the designation of being a CPA exists everywhere in the United States and usually, you can transfer your license from one jurisdiction to another. Job mobility is not only defined as your ability to move geographically but also the ability to advance within an organization as well as move to other organizations. As we discuss in chapter 4, the majority of CPAs will start their careers in accounting firms which are commonly referred to as *public accounting*. While in public accounting you will have a very set career path with promotions typically every two to three years until you either become a partner or move into a specific industry also known as *private accounting*. Most CPAs usually excel in private accounting settings using the knowledge and experience they gained while in a firm resulting in rapid advancement. A good CPA can easily rise through the ranks, ultimately becoming a Chief Financial Officer or Vice President of Finance. These positions customarily have excellent compensation and benefits packages, as well as stock options for publicly traded companies. It is not unheard of for privately held companies to offer their high ranking employees a chance to buy into the company.

Should you find that you have reached a ceiling in your current organization, it usually isn't tough to find another organization within the industry, offering a higher position at a better salary. It is not uncommon for placement firms seeking talented accountants to reach out via social media platforms like LinkedIn. I strongly recommend that you stay active within any professional organizations that you belong to and keep your profile updated on LinkedIn. Even if you are not actively looking to make a change, you never know when an amazing opportunity may come knocking at your door.

Flexible Working Schedule

The lack of flexibility used to be a major negative within the profession, especially when it came to working in public accounting. A request for a flexible schedule was viewed as a lack of dedication to the work and the firm. Luckily, times have changed. To attract and retain first rate employees, many firms have slowly come to realize that a certain amount of flexibility must be supported. Firms are more likely to offer much more flexibility throughout the rest of the year to compensate for the high work volume during tax season. Compensation may include the ability to work part time from home. Many firms close early or for the whole day on Fridays during off-peak seasons. However, don't expect to be offered the opportunity to work from home right away. You will need to gain some experience before being able to work independently. Someone who values flexibility and a certain sense of freedom may reject the constraints of a traditional firm; opting to go out on their own.

One of the ways that potential employers lure people away from public accounting into private accounting is with the promise of fewer hours and more flexibility. Working from home can be one of those lures. Advances in technology have made it simple for employees to handle business from the comfort of their home office. Working from home has some great benefits. It allows you to get the same amount of work done while avoiding the cost, both time and money, of the morning commute. The high demand for CPAs can make this a significant part of the negotiation process when seeking a position.

Working with Great People

If there were one aspect of being a CPA that I completely underestimated the value of in the beginning, it would be this one. Once you begin your journey toward becoming a CPA right until the end of your career, you will meet and work with many great people. It will start with some dynamite college professors and then coworkers, clients and the board of directors. In the early part of your professional career, do your best to work with people that are willing to teach and guide you. This will not only help you learn the profession but give you role models to emulate once you become the boss. You will likely find that your days in public accounting will provide you with lifelong contacts. As in any profession, there will be those people on power trips with egos that are much bigger than they are. Learn what you can from them but don't waste your time on them. While it may be part of their job to teach and supervise you, their personal goal is to make you feel inferior. Remember, they were once in your shoes and didn't have the knowledge that they have now. In your career, you will inevitably cross paths with damaged people; that's life. Try your best to look past these people and look to the positive personal experiences you are having.

Growth

One of the most important things to consider when deciding on a career path is securing employment in a growing industry. Seldom does a month go by when I'm not contacted by one or more associates who have an open position they are looking to fill.

Additionally, placement firms routinely call me on behalf of one or more clients looking for accountants with or without professional experience. There are plenty of jobs in this field, and the growth potential is tremendous. According to the United States Bureau of Labor Statistics in 2016 there were 1,397,700 jobs for accountants and auditors with an annual growth rate projected at 10% for the years 2016-2026 as compared to 7% for all occupations. This equates to an additional 139,900 jobs created during that period.

A major reason for this growth is that much of an accountant's job is focused on compliance. Our society appears to have become more focused on accountability inside and outside of virtually every organization, and thus monitoring becomes more of a priority. The financial crisis of 2008 has only fueled the governmental requirements and the need for accountants to audit organizations. Demands call for accountants to safeguard assets ensuring that people are working in the best interest of the organizations that they represent.

It's also safe to say that this profession will not be a victim of technology but rather it will create more opportunities within the business. The need for accountants to create and maintain complex computerized accounting systems continues to grow at a frantic pace. These systems also need a legion of people who understand how to use these systems, audit them and protect them from fraudulent activity. The movement to cloud based systems will only enhance the need for tech savvy accountants. This will naturally create opportunities for young accountants to step in and fill these roles. The hard truth is many older accountants aren't willing to put in the effort to learn these new systems. Generally speaking, younger people have more of an aptitude for technology as it has been a significant part of most of their lives. Older adults have had to learn it and are, in truth, less likely to embrace it.

Sense of Purpose

Unfortunately, many people spend their careers doing functions rather than performing work that adds real value to themselves and society. Accountants are the gatekeepers to more than the average person understands. So many ideas, plans, and projects need a CPA to turn them into reality. We analyze and monitor from a fiscal standpoint to make sure these projects are feasible and completed as planned. Walt

Disney was an amazing idea man, but it was his brother, Roy, who had the financial aptitude to make it all a reality.

In all likelihood, you will become a leader within the organization and, even in the industry should you choose to. You will be at the forefront of making decisions that will shape the future of that organization, set policies, and procedures, as well as mentor people. You may have the opportunity to sit on boards of charitable organizations that are meaningful to you. A point of caution here, make sure you choose boards that align with your interests and values and maintain the utmost ethical and moral standards. Choose wisely and do your homework to ensure that the organization selected is fiscally sound.

Good Benefits

Let me start this section by saying if you are a CPA or someone working toward licensure and don't have excellent benefits, then you are in the wrong organization and need to find employment elsewhere. With a shortage of qualified individuals, good employers know they have to offer competitive benefits packages, as well as compensation to attract excellent candidates. The financial team of any organization is often involved in the process of selecting employee insurance. This benefit is often overlooked. As a member of the financial team, you have a say in your benefits. Often quality health insurance isn't a focus of younger people entering the workforce. Having health insurance is extremely important. Keep in mind that it only takes one accident or unexpected illness to set a person back financially for a long time.

I speak from experience in this matter. I became very ill in my early 30's and when all was said and done, the medical bills totaled over $130,000! Without solid medical insurance, it's safe to say that I would still be paying those bills.

While it's important to consider the entire benefits package, it is also important to keep in mind the cost associated with being a CPA. In chapter 5, we will discuss in greater detail the cost license renewals, professional organizations, and continuing professional education credits (CPE). These costs can easily total over $1,000 per year, making it necessary to negotiate this part of your benefits package before accepting a position.

Making a Positive Impact on the World

In any country's population, there are a lot of negative feelings towards capitalism and its perceived effects on society. To a large number of people, the accounting profession is one that symbolizes capitalism and the greed associated with it. I would argue that accountants are the first line of defense in protecting people from the greed of others. We are the ones that audit organizations to ensure that the accounting records are accurate, and the individuals involved are maintaining financial integrity. Consider the last big fraud case you saw on the news. Who do you think was behind the scenes digging through the evidence and summarizing the results? An accountant.

While many politicians would have you believe that they are the protectors of your tax dollars, it's accountants who are the real gatekeepers. Whether working in public accounting or as an auditor within the government, the accountant is the one that safeguards the public's money. They analyze not only the financial workings of governmental units, but the projects funded by the government for many different activities, including those that benefit people on lower economic levels. They will ensure that these funds are spent as intended so that the people who need it the most reap the rewards. This also applies to municipal projects including roads, bridges, water, sewer, firehouses, and police stations to ensure public funds are maximized. They will also ensure that people working on these projects receive a fair wage, whether it be with a private contractor or a public worker. Accountants are instrumental in the issuing of public debt such as bond offerings and government backed mortgages. These enable projects to occur in the first place.

Behind any sizable charitable gift, there is an accountant who helped structured that gift to obtain the maximum benefit to the donor. The accountant will make sure that the donor receives appropriate tax incentives; encouraging the donor to give again and have the resources to do so. Additionally, he will work with attorneys to create trusts for wealthier individuals. These trusts will go on to benefit charities long after the donor has passed away. Accountants are in a great position to help charities, not only by serving on their boards, but by offering their services such as preparing tax filings for free.

While the great recession of 2008 hurt the credibility of the accounting profession to some degree, it is still among the most trusted jobs in the United States. There is a certain amount of status that comes with being a CPA as they are commonly considered to be smart, ethical, and professional individuals.

Conclusion

Choosing a major in college is never an easy task. Most high school students will change their minds several times before settling on one. Upon entering college, about 33 percent of students in the United States end up changing their major at least once in their first three years.[2] If you have already chosen a major and are contemplating a change to accounting, don't feel like you are alone in this thought process. Whatever you do, make sure to select a field of study that has a career path to it. There are countless college majors out there that don't lead to jobs that make the time and money invested in the college degree worth it. Don't feel that you have to be a math genius to be successful in the industry. While you may need to take some complicated math in college, you will probably never use most of it when you start working in the field.

This book will not only focus on the steps it takes to become a CPA but also the professional and financial benefits of being one. These steps are known in the industry as the 3 E's: college Education, passing the Exam, and obtaining Experience. In general, you will be required to take five years of college, pass a four-part exam, and have two years of professional experience. The specifics of these

---

[2] "Nearly a third of students change major within three years -- math ...." 8 Dec. 2017, https://www.insidehighered.com/news/2017/12/08/nearly-third-students-change-major-within-three-years-math-majors-most. Accessed 1 Sep. 2018.

requirements vary state to state, which I will outline in subsequent chapters.

Chapter 2 - Education Requirements

There are two separate sets of educational requirements that you need to be concerned with on your path to becoming a CPA. The first is the requirement to sit for the exam, and the second is becoming certified. Unfortunately, there are no national uniform standards. The exact process is left up to the 55 states and territories within the US, which are called jurisdictions. As you read through this chapter, I recommend that you refer to Appendix A for the requirements in your jurisdiction.

Each jurisdiction has a State Board of Accountancy that sets and monitors those educational standards. The State Boards belong to an organization called the National Association of State Boards of Accountancy (NASBA). The NASBA website serves as a great reference tool as well as providing contact information for all 55 jurisdictions. I strongly recommend that you contact your state board should you have questions regarding whether your college courses meet the requirements. While career colleges and some online programs have great value in the educational system sometimes their classes don't meet a jurisdiction's standards. College and university accounting programs are designed to meet the educational requirements within their jurisdiction and may not meet the criteria to sit for the exam in another jurisdiction. Better to check with your State Board first before committing to a program that doesn't meet eligibility requirements for your jurisdiction.

All jurisdictions in the United States (except for the U.S. Virgin Islands) require that you earn 150 credit hours from accredited colleges or universities to become certified.

They also require that a bachelor's degree is earned within those 150 credit hours. Each jurisdiction has specific requirements concerning how many of those credit hours need to be in accounting and other related classes. The State Board of Accountancy in your jurisdiction will review your application to ensure that you have met the educational requirements before being issued a CPA license.

To those readers who are still high school students: I highly recommend that you follow your school's college track curriculum. I encourage you to take math classes including college algebra, elementary statistics, business statistics, precalculus, and calculus. These are classes that college admissions departments will specifically look for on your high school transcript. Also, I see so many students enroll in college as accounting majors without ever taking a single business class in high school. This has always been a mystery to me. Please do yourself a favor and take whatever accounting and business law classes your high school has to offer. While these are basic level classes, they will give you a decent perspective as to whether you have the interest and aptitude to major in accounting on the college level.

So, you didn't get the best grades or pick the right courses in high school. Have no fear! There is a viable alternative. Start at a two-year college, earn your associate's degree in accounting or a closely related business program and then transfer to a four-year college. The following are some tips and benefits to attending an associate degree program before embarking on a bachelor's degree program;

- Be sure to select an associate degree program at a regionally or nationally accredited college. Typically, most or all the classes you take will count towards your 150-hour credit requirement.

- Attending a two year school first is a money saver! They tend to have lower tuition and fees than their four-year counterparts. Many students decide to live at home while attending these programs, which will save even more money on room and board.
- Many two year schools will have transfer agreements with four-year schools whereby any student that maintains a certain grade point average will be automatically be accepted into their program. Should there be a bachelor's degree program that you covet, check to see if there are any transfer agreements in place.
- Sometimes four-year schools will offer scholarships to transfer students that aren't available to students just coming out of high school. This is because transfer students typically have a higher graduation rate in bachelor's degree programs than their high school counterparts. Also, they can offer scholarships for only two years rather than the standard four years.
- An associate degree accounting program offers many of the core accounting classes required in a bachelor's degree program. This can help you decide if you have an aptitude and interest for this field of study before committing to a four-year program.
- If you decide after two years that college isn't for you will already have a degree and marketable skills.
- Keep in mind that you will get the same bachelor's degree regardless of where you started and will likely save a considerable amount of money in the process.

Should you choose the traditional route and decided right from the beginning to earn their Bachelor of Accounting, you will be required to earn 120 college credits. The majority of classes offered by a college are three-credit-hour courses. On average you will take five classes each semester over eight semesters. Most colleges have two semesters per year. This is why bachelor's degrees are customarily considered to be four year programs. While a college itself may be impressive, their accounting program may not be strong. Try not to base your decision on emotion but rather try to think like a consumer buying any other big ticket item. Remember, this will be one of the most significant financial investments of your life and you want to realize the maximum return on your investment. I recommend that you consider the following attributes when selecting a bachelor's degree in accounting program.

- The CPA exam pass rate among the program's alumni. This is usually advertised on the college's website. If the college doesn't have statistics available, you can search NASBA's website under the University Edition section.
- The job placement rate for graduates and more importantly, the types of jobs they secure. Make sure your employment goals match the types of jobs listed.
- Find out what kind of firms and companies interview on campus. It is always a positive sign when nationally recognized firms/companies are willing to recruit on campus. This is an indication that the school has a quality program and its graduates are in demand.
- Make sure the college is either regionally or nationally accredited to ensure that their classes will

meet the 150-hour credit requirement. This helps to ensure that your teachers are competent. The credentials of teachers in an accredited school are periodically reviewed as part of an overall peer review of the program itself. College websites will post their accreditation status as well as the results of their most recent peer reviews.

- Make inquiries regarding internship programs and the types of organizations involved in the program. Find out the placement rate for those participating in the program who go on to work at an organization for which they interned.
- Consider the number of students within the accounting program and how long it's been in existence. Smaller and newer programs ordinarily don't have the same positive reputation as their counterparts. Nor do they have extensive alumni networks that can serve you later as a great job placement tool.

If you have not earned a bachelor's or master's degree in accounting, five states still allow you to sit for the exam. Alaska, Georgia, Hawaii, Maine, and Massachusetts don't require an accounting degree yet have the 120 credit hour requirement. The courses needed for those programs will include several education courses as well as accounting/business courses. The specific course requirements for a degree will vary based on the college and the jurisdiction where it is located. Below is a listing and description of accounting/business courses typically required to earn a bachelor's degree in Accounting;

- **Financial Accounting** This is usually a student's first accounting course and will cover the fundamentals of accounting, as well as the basics for creating financial statements for external users such as owners, investors, and financial institutions. This course is the foundation for the majority of all the other accounting courses a student will take in their academic career.
- **Managerial Accounting** Likely to be the second accounting course taken and will cover the internal aspects of accounting within an organization such as product-costing systems, budgeting, profit evaluations, and reports to various levels of management.
- **Cost Accounting** This is somewhat of an extension of Managerial Accounting. It takes an in-depth look into using various costing systems to determine budgeting, costing, and profits for different types of products, services, and other activities.
- **Auditing** focuses on the planning, conducting and reporting of audits on financial statements to ensure that they aren't materially misstated and adhere to generally accepted accounting principles. Additionally, audits are used to ensure that the organization complies with internal control policies and procedures and that external financial regulations are being followed.
- **Accounting Information Systems** This course tends to vary in structure and content depending on the college. Essentially it

teaches the basics of accounting software systems to ensure accuracy and proper safeguards. Some colleges have predetermined software packages, while others have the student select the software based on a given set of criteria.

- **Intermediate Accounting** Many accounting students consider these the most challenging courses of all the accounting courses they take. The course takes an in-depth look at the theoretical concepts and financial statements while incorporating generally accepted accounting principles. This course is typically split into two parts that are taken consecutively during the fall and spring semesters.

- **Federal Taxation** provides an overview of federal income taxes for individuals, partnerships, and corporations. Students will analyze basic tax scenarios, research applicable tax laws and complete various federal tax returns.

- **Government and Not-for-Profit Accounting** introduces the principles and procedures used for government and not-for-profit organizations and will focus on fund accounting and budgetary procedures.

In addition to the required accounting courses, most colleges will require or recommend that you take courses in Microeconomics, Macroeconomics, Statistics, Marketing, Business Law, and Business Communications. I would strongly recommend that you also take Psychology and

Sociology courses as they are excellent at helping you understand people in business and social settings. While a career in accounting may appear to emphasize numbers, understanding, and interacting with people in the business world will contribute to your success in this field.

It is not uncommon to read the rule regarding earning 150 credit hours and automatically assume that they are required to earn their master's degree. While many do earn a graduate degree, it is **not** required by any of the jurisdictions. As I have outlined below, there are several ways to meet the 150-hour requirement. Regardless of the path you choose, make sure you earn the required accounting/business credits for your jurisdiction.

- As a cost-saving measure, consider getting your bachelor's in accounting and then taking the 30 additional credit hours of non-degree courses at a Community College to avoid the high cost of graduate courses.
- Consider a double major. A bachelor's in accounting with a minor in business or information systems could open more doors in a field that you would enjoy.
- Some colleges offer a bachelor's degree in accounting with an accelerated program in which you earn 150 credit hours and focus on preparing to sit for the exam.
- Should you receive your bachelor's in something other than accounting, it isn't too late to become a CPA. Simply earn a Master of Science in Accounting or a Master of Business Administration with a concentration in Accounting.

- Some colleges offer 5-year programs that are tailor-made to earn your bachelor's and master's degrees while receiving all the necessary credits.
- For many, the traditional route is preferred. Earn a bachelor's in accounting and then a Master of Science in an accounting related field.

Earning a graduate degree has a different set of standards that those of the undergraduate. Each graduate program will specialize in a particular area. The admissions process differs from that of gaining acceptance into an undergraduate program. In addition to the actual application, admission committees will require some or all of the following items depending on the college and the program you are applying for;

- An essay or personal statement regarding your reasons for applying to the program and why you believe that you will be a successful candidate.
- Letters of recommendation from your undergraduate professors, preferably in your area of study. Don't forget to request letters from any internships or jobs you have held.
- Some colleges require the candidate to interview with a panel of admissions committee members.
- Transcripts from all the colleges you have attended; even if you didn't earn a degree. The committee will focus on grades, the quality of the college and types of class attended.
- Extracurricular activities such as clubs, sports, professional organizations, and military service. Most colleges will require a standardized test. Depending on the program, it will either be the Graduate

Management Admission Test (GMATs) or the Graduate Record Exam (GREs). Both tests are valid for five years, have hundreds of testing sites throughout the country, are offered several times a year, and have excellent study materials available.

- o The GMATs consist of four sections; Integrated Reasoning, Quantitative, Verbal and Analytical Writing. This exam allows 3.5 hours to complete.
- o The GREs consists of six sections which cover Analytical Writing, Verbal Reasoning, and Quantitative Reasoning. Two parts are dedicated to each subject and have a time limit of 3.75 hours.

CPA candidates may enroll in either a Master of Science (MS) or a Master of Business Administration (MBA) program depending on the field of study of their undergraduate degree and their ultimate career goals. Be aware that the credit hour requirements for these programs can increase if you don't have the necessary prerequisite undergraduate classes as required by the program. Also, make sure that between both the undergraduate and graduate degrees, all jurisdiction required courses have been completed.

With only 150 credit hours required, the MS accounting programs have become very popular. You can earn your degree with 30 credit hours and complete the program in one year of full-time studies. Most bachelor's degrees require 120 credit hours. The addition of the MS degree will not only give you the required hours and a degree in a specialized area but will also help further prepare you for the exam. Some of the popular MS programs are in the fields of taxation, forensic accounting, financial accounting, corporate accounting, audit/assurance services, and accounting information systems.

MBA programs can be desirable to potential employers who are seeking college graduates that aspire to high-level management positions within an organization. There is a wide array of MBA programs with various concentrations and specialties from which to choose. A program that concentrates on accounting will prepare its students for careers that include chief financial officer, treasurer, or controller in an accounting firm, financial institution, governmental agencies, small business or a major corporation. The programs usually require a student to earn 48 -60 credits and are designed to be completed in two years of full-time studies. Some colleges offer "executive programs" that cater to working professionals and allow them to attend the program on a part-time basis.

Regardless of the path you have chosen, you will ultimately need to earn your bachelor's degree and 150 credit hours overall. This is a sizeable commitment of time and resources. The American Institute of Certified Public Accountants (AICPA) offers a **free** Student Affiliate Membership. The membership is available for full and part-time students enrolled in a domestic or non-US college or university.[3] Many of the discounts and publications are offered to both paying members and student members. More

---

[3] "AICPA Student Membership : ThisWayToCPA : AICPA."
https://www.thiswaytocpa.com/aicpa-student-membership/. Accessed 18 Jan. 2020.

importantly, there are pages and pages of exclusive scholarship opportunities. The AICPA and its members recognize the need for accountants and want to help students reach their goals; with the bonus of more professionals in the field. I strongly encourage you to take advantage of this program and all it has to offer. Sign up at
https://www.thiswaytocpa.com/aicpa-student-membership

Lastly, remember to enjoy your college experience. You will meet like-minded people and make lasting relationships, both personally and professionally. You are going to have some dynamite professors who have a vast amount of experience in the accounting and business world. Listen to them. They are there to prepare you for what lies ahead. Nobody knows better than those that have been there. Enjoy your college years socially. They can be a magical time in your life. Make sure to prioritize and don't lose sight of why you are in college - to get that degree!

Chapter 3 - The CPA Exam

While education and experience requirements may vary, the exam itself is the same throughout all 55 jurisdictions. Some jurisdictions require an additional Ethics exam. The exam is created, managed and scored by the American Institute of Certified Public Accountants (AICPA) and administered at Prometric test centers under the direction of the National Association of State Boards of Accountancy (NASBA). The exam is a computer-based test consisting of four sections that allow four hours each. Sections can be completed in any order you choose. A passing grade for each is section is 75, and all four sections must be passed within an 18-month rolling period. In other words, credit for any section passed is valid for 18 months from the date the section is taken. If all four parts are not successfully completed in 18 months, you will have to retake each of the sections that have expired. While there is no limit to the number of times you can take a section, you can't sit for it more than once per quarter. This is referred to as a testing window. Once all four parts of the exam have been successfully completed, they don't expire. However, special rules do apply to the separate ethics test. This will be discussed later in this chapter. There are four steps to apply for the exam:

- Apply online. Depending on your jurisdiction you will either apply through the State Board of Accountancy or the NASBA CPA Examination Services at http://nasba.org/stateboards/ and pay the required fees. If you are unsure where to register for your jurisdiction, start with the NASBA website.

- Submit your college transcripts. Once approved, you will receive your Authorization to Test (ATT). The ATT is valid for 90 days. Make sure to register for the exam promptly.
- Register for the exam. Registering is done through the NASBA website at which time you will be required to pay the exam fees. The cost is approximately $200 per section.
- Notice to Schedule (NTS) is issued. This pass allows you to schedule your exam date. This process usually takes 6-8 weeks for first-time applicants and 6-10 days for repeat applications. Keep in mind the NTS does have an expiration date that will vary based on jurisdiction.

Registering for the exam is simple. Go to the NASBA website referenced above, choose your jurisdiction, then enter the information provided on your NTS. This will enable you to select a date and a Prometric test center. There are over 3,000 centers worldwide that are usually open six days a week. You must select a date within a predetermined testing window - typically within the first 70 days of the calendar quarter. You may take any of the four sections during a testing window, but as mentioned before you cannot take the same section more than once in the same window. Each part of the exam is broken down into blocks called testlets. Testlets are comprised of multiple-choice questions, task-based simulations and written communications, and include both operational and pretest questions. The operational questions are scored while pretest questions are not scored. The pretest questions may be used in future examinations depending on the statistical outcome of the answers given. There is no way for the test taker to tell the difference between the two types of questions. A brief description of the four exam sections are as follows:

- Auditing and Attestation (AUD) will test a candidate's understanding of procedures in gathering and evaluating an organization's information for various types of engagements, including audits. It also focuses on ethics, professional responsibilities, knowledge of the subject matter, and the use of judgment to conclude an organization's practices and financial statements.
- Business Environment and Concepts (BEC) will test the candidate's knowledge in corporate governance, financial and operations management, informational technology, and various analysis. This section will also focus on professional responsibilities in assorted engagements, including conducting audits as well as preparing tax returns.
- Financial Accounting and Reporting (FAR) will test a candidate's knowledge in various standards and regulations set forth by the relevant governing bodies including the AICPA, U.S. Securities and Exchange Commission, the Financial Accounting Standards Board, the Governmental Accounting Standards Board, and the International Accounting Standards Board. It also tests your understanding of how to apply these standards to prepare financial statements in their proper formats.
- Regulation (REG) will test a candidate's knowledge in U.S. federal taxation, ethics and professional responsibilities related to tax services as well as various subjects within the field of business law including contracts, transactions, and debt structures.

The federal taxation portion will focus on property transactions, individuals, and various ways organizations are taxed.

While a passing score for each section is a 75, the exam is not scored traditionally. Scoring is based on 75 points earned rather than 75% of the questions being answered correctly. It is imperative that before you sit for a section, you are aware of how the scoring is weighted for each section. The AICPA's website is the best resource for the current breakdown. An appeal through the NASBA website can be made should you feel that your exam was scored incorrectly. Currently, about ten jurisdictions do not allow appeals. Also, be aware that there is a cost associated with this process and very rarely does a candidate get their score changed.

According to the AICPA, at least half the candidates who sit for a section of exam each quarter fail it. While this may sound discouraging it also means that approximately 50% will pass. Your chances for success are directly tied to your strategy and preparation. While there are companies that sell excellent exam review programs, it is crucial that you have a sound understanding of how each section of the exam is structured. I recommend that you review the website aicpa.org/cpaexam as it offers beneficial and free materials like blueprints of the exam, sample tests, and tutorial topics. The AICPA does a top-notch job of not only keeping the materials current but also informing candidates of upcoming changes in the content of each section.

Once you have reviewed the free materials provided by the AICPA, it's time to set forth a strategy for passing the exam. The 18-month time frame will go by faster than you think so consider the order in which you want to take the sections. While I don't recommend that you sit for all four parts during the same testing window, some candidates have been successful in this approach. Many successful candidates take a systematic approach to testing; completing one or two sections during each testing window. Considering that the clock starts when passing the first part of the exam, many candidates decide to take what they feel will be the hardest one first. Statistically, the hardest section of the exam is Financial Accounting and Reporting (FAR). Just as important as your strategy is your preparation for the exam. Preparing for the exam takes a lot more time than you may think. Plan accordingly. Several companies offer excellent review courses ranging anywhere from $1,000 to $3,000. I won't be endorsing any one company in this book. I suggest that you select a larger company that has been established in the industry for several years. These companies tend to have more resources to stay current with changing trends as well as the exam. One of the most challenging factors of studying for the exam is the large amount of material that could potentially be in each section. Review courses do their best to focus your time on those areas that they believe will be on the current year's exam.

Customarily, three different formats are offered by these review companies; in-person classroom settings, live online classes, or self-study. Candidates need to select the form that makes sense for them based on their work schedules and study habits. At this point in your life, you probably have a pretty good understanding of what type of learner you are and your general motivation. Some candidates need the structure of a classroom setting or live online classes while others are more content to work at their own pace in a self-study format. The other factor to consider is whether your current work schedule will enable you to attend classes in a classroom setting. If your job requires a lot of travel, you will need to select another study option. How long do you need to study? The consensus is 100-120 hours of study for each section. Keep this in mind when choosing a review type. You aren't alone in this challenge. There is a plethora of free "support groups" on social media. Here you can exchange ideas, answer each other's questions, and make lasting contacts for your professional career.

Approximately 35 jurisdictions will require you to take an ethics exam within two years of passing the CPA exam. It is designed to prepare candidates for ethical problems they might encounter in their public accounting careers. This test is also written and administered by the AICPA. It is not nearly as extensive as any section of the CPA exam. The exam is 40 multiple choice questions and can be taken online or in a paper format at home. If you decide to complete it online, you will find out your grade immediately while the paper format requires you to mail in the answer sheet and wait for the results. When you sign up for the exam, you will receive self-study materials from the AICPA. The cost $150-$200 for both the exam and study materials. Make sure you take the time to study for this test as a passing grade is 90%. You can retake the exam online up to three times. The fourth attempt will need to be submitted in written form. While not all jurisdictions currently require an ethics exam, the trend shows that most are adopting this requirement or will be in the future. Some jurisdictions will issue your CPA certificate upon passing the exam. You will then have to complete the experience requirements (discussed in Chapter 4) to get your license.

The rest of the jurisdictions require you to pass the exam and complete the experience requirements before they issue you both your certificate and license.

While the CPA exam is a significant commitment of time and resources, rest assured that it will be well worth it in the end. I have worked with many accountants throughout the years who didn't devote the time to the exam after college and therefore never became certified. While most of them have gone on to have good careers, they never reached their true earning potential. There is a certain amount of status in the business world that comes with being a CPA and it will open doors for you. Don't let the exam overwhelm you. Take a systematic approach in your strategy and preparation. Don't get discouraged if you don't pass a section the first time. Use any failures as a learning experience in your preparation for the next attempt. Try to take the exam during or shortly after your college career. Check with your jurisdiction to see what is allowed. A lot of what you learn in college will show up in the exam. The fresher in your mind they are, the better your chances of being successful. Don't let time slip away after college. You will thank yourself later. Trust me.

Chapter 4 - Experience Requirements

The majority of CPAs, myself included, fulfill their experience requirement in a public accounting firm. In these firms, you will work with other accountants providing accounting expertise, auditing, and tax services to a wide range of clients, including various size businesses, not-for-profit organizations, and governmental industries. While these jobs are demanding, especially during tax season, they provide you with a vast amount of professional experience. This experience would be nearly impossible to duplicate in any other setting. My experience in public accounting has shaped my entire career by teaching me not only accounting practices but the fundamentals of business. In this chapter, I will discuss the general structure of public accounting firms as well as the benefits and some pitfalls associated with working for them.

In any profession, one of the biggest challenges that job seekers face is getting the experience needed to get the position they want. You can't obtain experience without first having a job, and you can't get a job without having experience. A benefit of going into public accounting is the ready-made career path available for those coming out of college. Dues to a constant need to fill entry-level positions, firms of all sizes will send recruiters to college campuses to interview potential employees. There is a tremendous amount of turnover in this industry as accountants leave firms after fulfilling their experience requirements to take positions elsewhere. While public accounting can be very challenging with long hours and significant travel, it is a means to an end.

Public accounting firms are required to be owned by currently licensed CPA's.[4] Depending on the jurisdiction, the requirement could be anywhere from a simple majority to 100%. The owners are referred to as partners, and will specialize in either audit, tax or consulting services The financial benefits of becoming a partner are quite significant; salaries range well into the six figures depending on the size of the firm and the number of clients assigned to that partner. While this sounds great, only about two percent of those who enter public accounting will ever become partners. Unfortunately, many people leave their public accounting careers, feeling disappointed and sometimes bitter for not being elevated to partner positions. I recommend that you enter a public accounting firm with your eyes open to the fact that your ultimate career likely lies somewhere else. Treat this like a game of chess; enjoy the game but always be thinking about your next move.

While working in a public accounting firm, there are various levels that you will reach depending on your aptitude, work ethic, and the amount of time employed. In larger firms, you will likely be assigned to a specific department; for example, audit, tax, or consulting. There are typically three categories below the level of partner in public accounting:

- You will start as a staff accountant and spend approximately two to three years at this level and usually report to the senior accountant.

[4] "STATE NON-CPA OWNERSHIP PROVISIONS The Uniform ... - aicpa." https://www.aicpa.org/Advocacy/State/StateContactInfo/uaa/Download ableDocuments/Non-CPA_Ownership.pdf. Accessed 18 Jan. 2020.

○ If you are assigned to the auditing department, you will do a lot of detailed work such as testing financial transactions, reconciling accounts, and creating reports to summarize the results. Depending on the structure of your firm, you may also be asked to prepare tax returns. This will likely seem stressful but is an excellent opportunity for you to see how these organizations functional, both financially and operationally. You will have the benefit of having your work reviewed by the senior accountant or manager on the engagement. These review notes are invaluable. The reviewer's job is to make sure that you have done the work correctly and to help you to consider other aspects; to point out things you may not have thought of. This not only ensures that the work is precise for the client but can be viewed as a learning opportunity for you. Take these notes constructively, correct the errors, answer the questions, and learn from your mistakes. We have all had those moments when we thought we did an amazing job only to get pages of review notes back. While discouraging, it's fixable and is in the best interest of both you and the client.

- A tax staff accountant will prepare several different types of tax returns and be involved in basic tax planning and research issues. As with an audit staff accountant, you will receive review notes and learn a tremendous amount about the Federal and State tax systems.
- Consulting staff accountant duties aren't as easily defined. Their assignments will vary from one engagement to the next, depending on the specific needs of the client. If you like a variety, then this may be the department for you.

- The next stop along the way is a senior accountant. Most spend two or three years here and usually report to the manager.
  - When you are assigned to the auditing department, you will be the *boots on the ground* with the client; directing the audit fieldwork, supervising the staff accountants, and reviewing their workpapers. You will also likely be responsible for preparing financial statements, possibly reviewing tax returns and evaluating the client's internal controls.
  - A senior tax accountant will prepare or review tax returns for various types of organizations as well as tax planning and preparing different tax scenarios for clients.

- A senior consulting accountant will work under the direction of a manager or partner and will perform various duties based on the specifications of the engagement that has contracted between the firm and the client.
- The last stop (depending on how firms are structured) before partner, is the role of manager. Six or more years of experience are typically required to gain this position. Managers usually report directly to the partners.
  - An audit manager supervises staff and senior accountants on an engagement and is responsible for the day to day client contact, scheduling, billings, budgetary concerns, and staff evaluation. They also review the audit workpapers and approve the financial statement for partner review. Many times, they will have multiple projects occurring at the same time and therefore need to be diligent with their time.
  - A tax manager does many of the same tasks that a tax senior will perform but at a higher level. They are more likely to be the ones dealing with complex and unusual tax situations as well as higher-level tax research involving tax codes and previous court cases.
  - A consulting manager, much like an audit manager, will have the overall

responsibility for the engagement and will likely handle the more complex issues such as internal and operational control procedures.

Like businesses in any other industry, firms come in all different sizes that range from small, one office operations to international networks of firms operating under the same name. These are referred to as "The Big Four". These firms include Deloitte Touche, PricewaterhouseCoopers, Ernst & Young, and Klynveld Peat Marwick Goerdeler; all of which average between 25 to 35 billion dollars in revenue each year. Many graduating accounting students aspire to work for this type of firm because the pay is better, as are the opportunities to work with major companies around the globe. Working here can help to build relationships with business leaders and offer the accounting experience preferred by major corporations. While many college students find The Big 4 attractive for the reasons I have just mentioned, there are also great opportunities out there in the more than 46,000[5] small and mid-size firms. Before accepting an offer with a smaller firm, I recommend that you take a hard look at the type of clientele they service, including the size and type of industries. Make sure these are industries that interest you as this is where you will be spending your time.

---

[5] "Positions in Public Accounting - aicpa."
https://www.aicpa.org/career/careerpaths/publicaccounting.html.
Accessed 18 Jan. 2020.

The reason that I stress the choice of firms and thinking about the future is that many people leave a firm to go work for their clients. Often you will be assigned repeatedly to the same client. This usually indicates that you have an aptitude for the client's business, the firm is happy with your performance and/or they have specifically requested you. This creates a situation of familiarity between you and the client's organization regarding their accounting systems, organizational structure, operations, and management team. While you are working diligently on a client's books, you may unknowingly have been on a job interview for multiple years. Firms are typically supportive of their clients hiring the firm's employees as they feel that it gives them a better chance of retaining that client for future years. Remember only 2% of us will ever become partners so the rest of us need a path to our next career adventure.

I worked at a mid-sized firm for five years. This was a remarkable experience both personally and professionally for me. I was assigned to the audit department which also did the tax returns for its clients. I was able to get experience in both audit and tax. The clients that I had the pleasure of working with ranged in all types of industries, including healthcare, higher education, real estate, manufacturing, not-for-profits plus various local, state and federal governmental entities. I got paid to travel all over the country staying in incredible cities and meeting a vast array of leaders in business and government. The one thing that I always caution accountants working in firms is not to leave too soon. I worked my way up to the position of manager, and it wasn't until I spent some time in that role did, I feel that I was fully prepared to obtain and succeed at a higher-level position in private accounting. Many of my associates left firms after a couple of years. I believe that this set them back in the long run. It took them more time to move through the ranks in private accounting. If they had stayed a couple more years in public accounting, they might have seen greater success.

I'm sure you are asking yourself why I ever left public accounting after telling you what a tremendous opportunity it was for me. Like most things in life, you just know when it's time to move on. My wife was pregnant with our first child, and the traveling was exciting, but it wasn't conducive to me being the type of dad I wanted to be. The firm was already top-heavy with partners, and I didn't see any real path to further advancement with them. I took a job with one of the firm's healthcare clients as their controller; which was basically the head of their accounting department. That job served as a launching pad for me into a more prominent healthcare organization where I eventually became the Chief Financial Officer and a minority owner. Looking back, I'm confident that it was the right decision as I had already worked with several of healthcare organizations during my time in public accounting and felt comfortable in my knowledge of the industry.

Experience requirements vary based on jurisdiction as shown in Appendix A. Some of them strictly require that you spend one to two years working in public accounting while others will allow you to get your experience in other fields. The fact that public accounting firms offer such a wide range of tasks and opportunities it is a universally acceptable form of experience. It is important to understand that regardless of the path you choose ultimately a currently licensed CPA will have to sign off on your experience. In some jurisdictions, you will need to be supervised directly by a CPA while others allow a CPA to sign off on an experience affidavit if they are reasonably familiar with a candidate's work and performance. While working in public accounting, you will be supervised by one or more CPA's, making it easy for them to sign off. Other fields can be challenging based on who is managing you and what the specific rules are within your jurisdiction. It is best to contact the NASBA and discuss the matter with your employer before you start.

Whatever path you choose to fulfill your experience requirements do your best to enjoy the ride. Starting your professional career can be stressful. You may feel lost from time to time, but you will be surrounded by people with vast amounts of experience. Take advantage of that. This is truly a time of personal enlightenment as you have the opportunity to learn from some of the best people you will ever work within your career. Most professionals who are assigned new staff remember what it was like to be in your shoes and will evaluate you based on your overall effort and your ability to grasp concepts and apply them. These experiences are laying the foundation for the rest of your career. Most of us look back and realize they were some of the best days of our professional career, we just didn't know it at the time.

Chapter 5 - After you Become a CPA

Once you become certified, there are ongoing costs to keep your license current, and you updated in a profession of ever changing trends and regulations. Like most of the aspects of becoming a CPA, the rules vary based on your jurisdiction when it comes to license renewal and the continuing professional education (CPE) requirements. There will be a cost for memberships to any of the professional organizations you are eligible to join. This chapter will give you an overview of these costs. Remember, it is possible to negotiate the coverage of these fees with your future employer during the hiring process. Many CPA firms will pay for them as part of your overall compensation package. In private accounting this is not the case. This will need to be part of the compensation discussion.

Your initial certification will be good for a period of one, two, or three years depending on your jurisdiction. Before your certification expires, you will receive a renewal notice. This notice will ask questions regarding any changes in demographics, any criminal convictions, as well as CPE requirement adherence. You will also be required to submit a renewal fee that covers the administrative cost of recording and maintaining licensure information. While most jurisdictions won't require you to provide evidence that you obtained the mandated CPE credits, they will have you sign an affidavit verifying this.

The most expensive and time consuming part of maintaining your CPA license is earning your CPE credits. The vast majority of jurisdictions require an average of 40 units of CPE each calendar year. A CPE credit is commonly a 50-minute block of time on topics that include, but are not limited to, accounting, auditing, ethics, governmental, nonprofit, management and taxes. Most jurisdictions allow you to choose your own topics but will require you to take two to six units of ethics during each licensing period. Continuing Education is usually structured into four or eight units but can be shorter or longer depending on the course design. Some courses are offered as self-study, either online or as printed materials and will require you to pass a test to receive credit. Other courses are offered in a traditional classroom type setting and are often part of a conference that will include several courses from which to choose over a period of days. These courses usually don't have a test at the end. Attendance of the course is sufficient.

When selecting CPE courses, it is vital that you make sure they are accepted by your jurisdiction. There are many companies out there that offer courses both online and in classroom settings. They will disclose how many credits a course is worth for each jurisdiction and if not check with them before buying a course. The cost of a CPE commonly ranges from $20 to $125 per credit. You don't want to invest the time and money into a course only to find out later that it doesn't meet your jurisdiction's qualifications. Once you complete a course, the provider will issue you a Certificate of Completion. This certificate will include the provider, course name, date and the number of CPE credits. This serves as proof that you have successfully completed the course.

One of the ways to save money on CPE and have access to a wide selection of acceptable courses is to join the American Institute of Certified Public Accountants (AIPCA). They have a vast collection of online classes and some interesting conferences which are held all around the country and are discounted for members. Their annual dues range from $150 to $475 depending on your job and industry.[6] There are also many other benefits to being a member including access to malpractice, auto, homeowners, business and life insurance. Additionally, they have agreements with several companies to provide discounts to their members in travel, technology, business services, and equipment. They also do a great job of keeping members up to date on news and trends within the industry through publications and postings on their website.

In addition to being a member of the AICPA, many CPA's belong to their own state societies of CPAs. Each of the 50 States as well as Washington D.C., Puerto Rico, the Virgin Islands, and Guam have these independent professional societies.[7] While each society is unique, they all serve as another good source for discounted CPE courses. These groups host conferences for their members to earn CPE credits. They also form committees or panel discussions to talk about issues affecting their jurisdiction. These societies also advocate in matters with state legislatures including tax issues and regulations involving professional standards. There is an annual membership fee. This can be an awesome opportunity to network with fellow CPA's in your area.

---

[6] "Annual Membership Dues - aicpa." https://www.aicpa.org/membership/dues.html. Accessed 18 Jan. 2020.
[7] "State Societies of CPAS | Encyclopedia.com." https://www.encyclopedia.com/finance/finance-and-accounting-magazines/state-societies-cpas. Accessed 23 Jan. 2020.

There are a large number of organizations that CPA's belong to which focus on specific areas of the profession, such as auditing, management, taxes, small businesses, and other specialties. These groups can be a great source of information and another great way to get discounted CPE credits that apply to your area of expertise. Once you leave public accounting you will likely find that whatever industry you are in will have some type of financial management association. These groups are comprised of senior level accountants from various organizations within that industry. They can be a great way to network and earn CPE credits that are designed for your field. You will also find it surprising how much assistance most of these individuals are willing to give in helping you face challenges within the industry. Remember the people that will be of the most help to you in your professional career are the ones that are dealing with the same challenges you are.

You have done all this work to earn your license and are maintaining it. Now let's talk about how to hold on to it. Occasionally, I will review the disciplinary actions against CPA's listed on the AICPA's website.[8] It baffles me how an individual could go through all the work and expense only to do something foolish and have their license suspended or even revoked. You will likely be faced with some ethical dilemmas in your career in which you will be faced with tough choices. Don't be afraid to walk away from a situation, rather than making the wrong decision. The reward is nowhere near the risk you are taking. I have personally known CPA's that lost their licenses in an attempt to make a

[8] "Disciplinary Actions - aicpa."
https://www.aicpa.org/forthepublic/disciplinaryactions.html. Accessed 18 Jan. 2020.

quick buck. The consequences of their future earning ability have been devastating. Remember how hard you have worked to reach this point. Below are the primary ways that CPA's lose their licenses[9];

- Failure to file a tax return
- Filing a fraudulent tax return on behalf of themselves or a client
- Failure to abide by the U.S. tax codes
- Conviction of a felony or any crime punishable by more than one year in prison
- Gross negligence
- Acts of fraud and dishonesty
- Fraudulently obtaining fees

As you can see from reading this book, becoming a CPA certainly doesn't happen overnight. It takes a lot of hard work and dedication to achieve this incredible goal. Looking back on it, I can honestly say that it was worth every moment of studying and the long hours I worked at the CPA firm. Once again, this certification can open doors personally and professionally that you cannot imagine. I genuinely hope that you will consider this field and it brings you all the personal and professional satisfaction that it has brought me.

---

[9] "Hold Onto Your CPA License: Ethical Issues To Avoid | Tampa ...." 6 Sep. 2017, https://www.davidrankinlaw.com/hold-onto-your-cpa-license-ethical-issues-to-avoid/. Accessed 15 Mar. 2019.

Appendix A - Educational & Experience [10]

This Appendix includes the educational, hours in accounting, accounting experience, and ethics exam requirements to become a licensed CPA in 55 jurisdictions. It also includes the requirements to sit for the exam which often differ from the licensure requirements. Please note that these are requirements as of January 18, 2020 therefore the CPA candidate should always check the website of their state board for updates.

---

[10] "Become a CPA - aicpa."
https://www.thiswaytocpa.com/licensure/state-requirements/.
Accessed 18 Jan. 2020.

Alabama

Education Requirements for Licensure	B.A. (120 hours)
Hours Required in Accounting for Licensure	120 semester hours of postsecondary education, including a baccalaureate degree at a regionally accredited college or university. 24 semester hours (excluding introductory courses) at the upper division undergraduate and/or graduate level *OR* Awarded a graduate degree in accounting from a Board-recognized program. Also required to sit for the exam: 24 semester hours in business courses (other than accounting courses) at the undergraduate or graduate level from among the following subject areas: economics; legal and social environment of business; business law; marketing; finance; organization, group, and individual behavior; quantitative applications in business; communication skills, and business ethics.
Exam Sitting Requirements	B.A. (120 hours)
Accounting Experience Requirements for Licensure	1 year public accounting or 2 years in industry, business, government, or college teaching
Ethics Exam	Must pass AICPA Ethics Exam for initial licensure.

Alaska

Education Requirements for Licensure	150 hours (including B.A)
Hours Required in Accounting for Licensure	24 semester credit hours of accounting courses. Also required: 9 total semester credit hours of business law, economics, and college math/computer science.
Exam Sitting Requirements	B.A. (120 hours) or equivalent or within 18 semester hours of completing a B.A.; must have completed 15 semester hours in accounting or one year of supervised accounting experience. Note: Advanced degrees are not accepted in lieu of a B.A.
Accounting Experience Requirements for Licensure	2 years accounting experience in government, industry, academia, or public practice verified by a supervising CPA.
Ethics Exam	Must pass AICPA Professional Ethics Exam for initial licensure

Arizona

Education Requirements for Licensure	150 hours (including B.A)
Hours Required in Accounting for Licensure	36 semester hours (30 hours must be in upper-level). Also required for licensure: at least 30 hours in related courses, including Business administration, Statistics, Computer science, information systems or data processing, Economics, Finance, Management, Business law, College algebra or more advanced mathematics, Advanced written communication, Advanced oral communication, General ethics, Marketing, and other courses closely related to the subject of accounting and satisfactory to the Board.
Exam Sitting Requirements	B.A. or higher (120 hours). Must have 24 semester hours of nonduplicative accounting courses, of which 12 semester hours are upper-level courses, and 18 semester hours in related courses.
Accounting Experience Requirements for Licensure	At least 2,000 hours in the practice of accounting. Experience must be sufficient to demonstrate the applicant's ability for critical inquiry and analysis of financial accounting information, including balance sheets, income statements, cash flow statements and tax returns and the applicant's ability to communicate, either orally or in writing, on the results of an inquiry or analysis of that information to an employer, client or a third party.
Ethics Exam	Must pass AICPA Professional Ethics Exam for initial licensure

Arkansas

Education Requirements for Licensure	150 hours (including B.A.)
Hours Required in Accounting for Licensure	30 upper-level hours, 20 graduate hours or a combination of both. Classes must cover Financial Accounting (Intermediate Acct.), Management Accounting (Cost Acct.), Governmental or Not-for-Profit Accounting (Institutional Acct.), Federal Taxation (Adv. Income Tax or Fundamentals of Taxation), Auditing and Attestation, and Accounting Information Systems.
Exam Sitting Requirements	120 hours (including B.A.)
Accounting Experience Requirements for Licensure	1 year experience, verified by a licensed CPA, through employment in government, industry, academia or public practice providing any type of services or advice involving the use of accounting, attest, management advisory, financial advisory, tax or consulting skills.
Ethics Exam	None

California

Education Requirements for Licensure	150 hours (including B.A)
Hours Required in Accounting for Licensure	24 semester units. Also required for licensure: 24 semester units of business-related subjects, 20 semester units of accounting study, and 10 semester units of ethics study.
Exam Sitting Requirements	120 hours (including B.A.) with 24 semester units in accounting and 24 semester units in business-related subjects.
Accounting Experience Requirements for Licensure	12 months of general accounting experience providing any type of service or advice involving the use of accounting, attest, compilation, management advisory, financial advisory, tax, or consulting skills. Qualifying experience may be gained through employment in public, private industry, or government. Experience acquired in academiais considered qualifying toward general accounting experience if the requirements of CBA Regulations section 12.1 are met.
Ethics	Must pass PETH examination administered by the California CPA (CalCPA) Education Foundation for initial licensure.

Colorado

Education Requirements for Licensure	150 hours (including B.A.)
Hours Required in Accounting for Licensure	33 semester hours of non-duplicative accounting coursework at the undergraduate or graduate level with course grades of C (or equivalent) or greater. 27 semester hours must be in accounting courses (excluding introductory accounting courses) covering specific subject areas. A total of 6 semester hours must be in auditing, which must include a 3 semester hour, or more, course concentrating on U.S. Generally Accepted Auditing Standards (GAAS). 3 semester hours, or more, must also be in a course concentrating on accounting or business ethics.
Exam Sitting Requirements	120 hours (including B.A.) with 27 semester hours of non-duplicative accounting coursework at the undergraduate or graduate level with course grades of C (or equivalent) or greater. The 27 hours must include 21 semester hours of accounting courses in particular subject areas (excluding introductory accounting courses) and a 3 semester hour auditing course concentrating on U.S. GAAS. Additionally, candidates must have 21 semester hours of non-duplicative coursework in business administration at the undergraduate or graduate level. No more than 6 of those hours can be in a single subject area.
Accounting Experience Requirements for Licensure	1 year of experience (or 1,800 hours) in Public Accounting, Industry, Government or Academia verified by an active CPA in good standing.
Ethics Exam	Must pass AICPA Professional Ethics exam for initial licensure.

Connecticut

Education Requirements for Licensure	150 hours (including B.A.)
Hours Required in Accounting for Licensure	36 semester hours. *Also required for licensure: 30 semester hours in economics & business administration, 60 semester hours in general education and 24 semester hours in any credit subject.
Exam Sitting Requirements	B.A. (120 hours) with 46 semester hours in accounting and related subjects, including, but not limited to business law, economics, and finance; at least 24 of those semester hours must be in accounting specifically.
Accounting Experience Requirements for Licensure	2 years in public practice, government or industry providing services or advice involving the use of accounting, attest, management advisory, tax or consulting skills all of which was supervised by a licensed certified public accountant or public accountant unless otherwise specified.
Ethics Exam	Must pass AICPA Ethics exam for initial licensure.

Delaware

Education Requirements for Licensure	150 hours (B.A.)
Hours Required in Accounting for Licensure	24 semester hours of courses in accounting principles, intermediate accounting, cost accounting, tax, auditing, advanced accounting, accounting information systems, and law.
Exam Sitting Requirements	B.A. (120 hours)
Accounting Experience Requirements for Licensure	1 year, verified by an active CPA, providing any type of services or advice using accounting, attest, compilation, management advisory, financial advisory, tax or consulting skills.
Ethics Exam	Must pass AICPA Ethics exam for initial licensure.

District of Columbia

Education Requirements for Licensure	150 hours (including B.A.)
Hours Required in Accounting for Licensure	24 semester hours that include financial accounting, auditing, cost accounting, and federal income taxes and 3 hours in commercial law.
Exam Sitting Requirements	120 hours (including B.A.) with 24 hours of accounting-related subjects and 3 hours of business law.
Accounting Experience Requirements for Licensure	1 year of experience, verified by an active CPA, providing any type of business services or advice using accounting, attest services, compilation, management advisory, financial advisory, tax, or consulting skills in government, industry, academia or public practice.
Ethics Exam	No ethics exam

Florida

Education Requirements for Licensure	150 hours (including B.A.)
Hours Required in Accounting for Licensure	30 semester hours of upper-division accounting covering taxation, auditing, financial and cost/managerial. Also required for licensure: 36 semester hours in upper division business courses that include 3 semester hours (or 4 quarter hours) of business law.
Exam Sitting Requirements	120 hours (including B.A.)
Accounting Experience Requirements for Licensure	1 year experience, verified by a licensed CPA, providing any type of service or advice involving the use of accounting, attest, compilation, management advisory, financial advisory, tax, or consulting skills in government, industry, academia, or public practice.
Ethics Exam	No ethics exam

Georgia

Education Requirements for Licensure	150 hours (including B.A.)
Hours Required in Accounting for Licensure	30 semester hours above the introductory level. Also required for licensure: 24 semester hours in business related subjects.
Exam Sitting Requirements	B.A. (120 hours)
Accounting Experience Requirements for Licensure	1 year and 2,000 hours in public accounting; 1 and 2,000 hours in business, industry, government or college teaching (teaching at a 4 year college or university in at least two different areas of accounting above the introductory or elementary level); or a combination of work experience in public accounting, business, industry, government or college teaching. All work experience must have been supervised by a person who holds a live permit as a certified public accountant except for government or college teaching. In these two areas you must be supervised; however, the supervisor is not required to hold a CPA license.
Ethics Exam	No ethics exam

Guam

Education Requirements for Licensure	Candidate must meet one of four educational requirement: Graduate degree w/a concentration in accounting or Graduate degree and complete 24 semester or equivalent quarter hours in accounting at the upper or graduate level or 150 hours (BA degree) from a business school or college of business and complete 24 hours in accounting at the upper or graduate level and 24 hours in business at the upper or graduate level or 150 hours (BA degree) from an accredited educational institution and 24 hours in upper or graduate level accounting and 24 hours of upper division or graduate level business
Hours Required in Accounting for Licensure	24 credit hours consists of upper division accounting courses, including the following courses: 3 credit hours in Financial Accounting, 3 credit hours in Auditing, 3 credit hours in Taxation, 3 credit hours in Management or Cost Accounting. 24 credit hours in business consists of courses: 6 credit hours in Economics, 3 credit hours in Finance, 3 credit hours in Business Law
Exam Sitting Requirements	120 hours - Transcript acknowledging BA degree or that following the examination the candidate is within 150 days of completion of the degree.
Accounting Experience Requirements for Licensure	Sat for exam November 2000 or after: 1 year experience in practice of public accounting gained through employment in government, industry, academia or public practice. Education exemption: If B.A. degree (with accounting concentration) was obtained and exam taken May 2000 or prior, 1 year of experience in public accounting will satisfy the experience requirement. Sat for exam May 2000 or prior: 2 years experience in practice or public

	accounting gained through employment in government, industry, academia or public practice.
Ethics Exam	No ethics exam

Hawaii

Education Requirements for Licensure	150 hours (including B.A.)
Hours Required in Accounting for Licensure	24 semester hours in upper division or graduate level accounting which would include courses in financial accounting, auditing, taxation and managerial accounting.
Exam Sitting Requirements	B.A. or within 120 days of B.A.
Accounting Experience Requirements for Licensure	1500 hours in audit, or 2-years in government, industry, academia, or public practice.
Ethics Exam	No ethics exam

Idaho

Education Requirements for Licensure	**150 hours (including B.A.)**
Hours Required in Accounting for Licensure	24 semester hours or equivalent quarter hours in accounting or 15 semester hours or equivalent quarter hours in accounting at graduate level
Exam Sitting Requirements	**B.A. (120 hours)**
Accounting Experience Requirements for Licensure	1 year experience in government, industry, public practice or academia.
Ethics Exam	Must pass AICPA Professional Ethics Exam for initial licensure or exam as approved by the Board of Accountancy

Illinois

Education Requirements for Licensure	150 hours (including B.A. or graduate degree)
Hours Required in Accounting for Licensure	*OPTION 1: If you earn at least a graduate degree in accounting from a regionally accredited institution or approved equivalent institution and AACSB or ACBSP accredited accounting program, there are no specific requirements for accounting or business hours. *OPTION 2* If you earn at least a graduate degree in business from a regionally accredited institution or approved equivalent institution and AACSB or ACBSP accredited business program, you must have completed 30 Semester Credit Hours (SCH) in accounting including Managerial Accounting, Taxation, Financial Accounting, Audit (no specific business hours requirement). *OPTION 3* If you earn at least a baccalaureate degree in any concentration or graduate degree with a concentration other than accounting or business from a regionally accredited institution or approved equivalent institution, you must have completed 30 SCH in accounting including Managerial Accounting, Taxation, Financial Accounting, Audit. You must also have completed 24 SCH in business including 2 SCH of Business Communication and 3 SCH of Business Ethics.
Exam Sitting Requirements	150 hours (including B.A. or higher)
Accounting Experience Requirements for Licensure	1 year of full-time experience, or its equivalent, providing any type of service or advice involving the use of accounting, attest, management advisory, financial advisory, tax, or consulting skills, which may be gained through employment in government, industry, academia, or public practice.
Ethics Exam	Must pass AICPA Professional Ethics Exam for initial licensure

Indiana

Education Requirements for Licensure	150 hours (including B.A.)
Hours Required in Accounting for Licensure	24 semester hours or equivalent quarter hours in undergraduate accounting or 15 semester hours or equivalent quarter hours in graduate level accounting or a equivalent combination of both
Exam Sitting Requirements	24 semester hours or equivalent quarter hours in undergraduate accounting or 15 semester hours or equivalent quarter hours in graduate level accounting or a equivalent combination of both
Accounting Experience Requirements for Licensure	2 years' experience in government, industry, academia or public practice.
Ethics Exam	No ethics exam

Iowa

Education Requirements for Licensure	150 hours (including B.A.)
Hours Required in Accounting for Licensure	24 semester hours or equivalent quarter hours in accounting above elementary level accounting or principles of accounting
Exam Sitting Requirements	B.A. or within 120 days of B.A.
Accounting Experience Requirements for Licensure	1 year experience in more than one employment situation (includes internships) in government industry, academia or public accounting. 2 years' experience for attest CPA which includes 1 year of attest and year of general experience.
Ethics Exam	Must pass AICPA Professional Ethics Exam for initial licensure

Kansas

Education Requirements for Licensure	150 hours (including B.A.)
Hours Required in Accounting for Licensure	30 semester hours or equivalent quarter hours in accounting theory and practice
Exam Sitting Requirements	150 hours (must complete education requirement prior to sitting for exam)
Accounting Experience Requirements for Licensure	1 year of accounting experience in government, industry, academia or public practice.
Ethics Exam	Must pass AICPA Professional Ethics Exam for initial licensure

Kentucky

Education Requirements for Licensure	150 hours (including B.A.)
Hours Required in Accounting for Licensure	27 semester hours or equivalent quarter hours in accounting
Exam Sitting Requirements	B.A (120 hours)
Accounting Experience Requirements for Licensure	1 year experience in an accounting or auditing position in public practice, academia, industry or government
Ethics Exam	No ethics exam

Louisiana

Education Requirements for Licensure	150 hours (including B.A.)
Hours Required in Accounting for Licensure	24 semester hours or equivalent quarter hours in accounting
Exam Sitting Requirements	Bachelor's degree (with core 24 hours of accounting courses and 24 hours of business courses)
Accounting Experience Requirements for Licensure	1 year experience in government, industry, academia or public practice.
Ethics Exam	No ethics exam

Maine

Education Requirements for Licensure	150 hours (including B.A.)
Hours Required in Accounting for Licensure	15 semester hours or equivalent quarter hours in accounting, auditing & ethics (3 hours must be in accounting and 3 hours must be in auditing)
Exam Sitting Requirements	B.A, or completion of B.A. within 120 days
Accounting Experience Requirements for Licensure	2 years of public accounting experience which must include the use of accounting or auditing skills including the issuance of reports on financial statement and at least one of the following: the provision of management advisory services, financial advisory services or consulting services, the preparation of tax returns, the furnishing of advice on tax matters
Ethics Exam	No ethics exam

Maryland

Education Requirements for Licensure	150 hours (including B.A.)
Hours Required in Accounting for Licensure	30 undergraduate semester hours in accounting and ethics subject matter, including: one 3 semester credit hour course each in auditing, cost accounting or managerial accounting, U.S. federal income tax and ethics; a minimum of 9 semester hour credits in financial accounting; and a minimum of 9 semester hour credits in elective accounting courses. Additionally, must have least 21 undergraduate semester hours completed in at least in five of the following nine subject areas: statistics, economics, corporation or business finance, management, marketing, U.S. business law, business communication, quantitative methods, and computer science/information systems.
Exam Sitting Requirements	B.A. Degree (120 hours) in accounting or its equivalent.
Accounting Experience Requirements for Licensure	1 year of experience, verified by a licensed CPA, providing any type of services or advice using accounting, attest, management advisory, financial advisory, tax or consulting skills.
Ethics Exam	Must pass AICPA Professional Ethics Exam for initial licensure

Massachusetts

Education Requirements for Licensure	150 hours (including B.A.)
Hours Required in Accounting for Licensure	30 undergraduate semester hours or 18 graduate hours covering financial accounting, auditing, taxation, and management accounting. Also required: 24 undergraduate semester hours or 18 graduate semester hours of business courses (other than accounting courses), or an equivalent combination thereof.
Exam Sitting Requirements	B.A degree (120 hours) including 21 credits in accounting that include coverage in financial accounting, audit, management accounting and taxation. Must also complete 9 credits in business courses that include information systems, finance, and business law.
Accounting Experience Requirements for Licensure	1 year of experience at a public firm or 3 years of experience at a non-public firm (industry, government, academia or nonprofit), verified by a licensed CPA, providing any type of services or advise using accounting attest, compilation, management advisory, financial advisory, tax and consulting skills.
Ethics Exam	No ethics exam

Michigan

Education Requirements for Licensure	150 hours (including B.A.)
Hours Required in Accounting for Licensure	B.A. degree 30 semester hours or equivalent quarter hours in accounting. M.A. degree in accounting or business-12 semester hours or equivalent quarter hours in graduate level accounting.
Exam Sitting Requirements	B.A. (120 hours) must be completed within 30 days following the actual date the candidate takes the first exam section.
Accounting Experience Requirements for Licensure	1 year of qualifying experience gained through employment in government, industry, academia or public practice.
Ethics Exam	No ethics exam

Minnesota

Education Requirements for Licensure	150 hours (including B.A.)
Hours Required in Accounting for Licensure	Graduate degree from a business school with 24 semester hours or equivalent quarter hours in undergraduate or 15 hours in graduate level accounting or B.A. or higher degree with 24 semester hours or equivalent quarter hours in accounting at the upper or graduate level
Exam Sitting Requirements	B.A. or completion of B.A. within 120 days
Accounting Experience Requirements for Licensure	1 year experience in public practice, government, industry or academia.
Ethics Exam	Must pass AICPA Professional Ethics Exam for initial licensure

Mississippi

Education Requirements for Licensure	150 hours (including B.A.)
Hours Required in Accounting for Licensure	24 semester hours or equivalent quarter hours in upper level or graduate level accounting (3 hours each must be in financial accounting, auditing, taxation, management/cost accounting and government/not-for-profit accounting)
Exam Sitting Requirements	150 hours (must complete education requirement prior to sitting for exam)
Accounting Experience Requirements for Licensure	1 year general experience of accounting and auditing skills, excluding academia.
Ethics Exam	No ethics exam

Missouri

Education Requirements for Licensure	150 hours (including a baccalaureate degree)
Hours Required in Accounting for Licensure	33 semester hours or equivalent quarter hours in accounting (1 course must be auditing, and 18 hours must be in upper level accounting; 27 semester hours in general business courses (i.e., marketing, management, economics, finance, etc.)
Exam Sitting Requirements	Must be within 60 days of completing education requirement
Accounting Experience Requirements for Licensure	1 year accounting experience in industry, government, academia or public practice. To sign reports or supervise attest services, the CPA will need 1 additional year of experience in attest work.
Ethics Exam	Complete written exam in professional ethics acceptable to the Missouri Board

Montana

Education Requirements for Licensure	150 hours (including B.A.)
Hours Required in Accounting for Licensure	24 semester hours above the introductory level to include one course each in financial accounting, auditing, taxation, and management accounting. Also required to sit for the exam: 24 semester hours in non-accounting general business courses.
Exam Sitting Requirements	120 hours (B.A. Degree)
Accounting Experience Requirements for Licensure	1 year having performed accounting and auditing functions ordinarily required in the practice of public accounting in the area of private, governmental, academic, or public accounting.
Ethics Exam	Must pass AICPA Professional Ethics Exam for initial licensure.

Nebraska

Education Requirements for Licensure	150 hours (including B.A.)
Hours Required in Accounting for Licensure	30 semester hours or equivalent quarter hours in accounting beyond principles of accounting
Exam Sitting Requirements	150 hours (must complete education requirement prior to sitting for exam)
Accounting Experience Requirements for Licensure	2 years of public accounting experience or 3 years of auditing experience in the Dept. of Revenue or in the Office of the Auditor of Public Accounts or 3 1/2 years gained through employment by the federal government as a special agent or IRS agent.
Ethics Exam	Must pass AICPA Professional Ethics Exam for initial licensure

Nevada

Education Requirements for Licensure	150 hours (including B.A.)
Hours Required in Accounting for Licensure	30 semester hours or equivalent quarter hours above the introductory level
Exam Sitting Requirements	150 hours (must complete education requirement prior to sitting for exam)
Accounting Experience Requirements for Licensure	2 years of public accounting experience in accounting or auditing, finance, advising or consulting with clients on matters relating to management, preparation of tax returns or the furnishing of advice on matters relating to taxes; or 4 years' experience in internal audit or governmental accounting and auditing considered to be substantially equivalent in the Board's judgment.
Ethics Exam	Must pass an ethics exam within the past 3 years that was approved by the Board

New Hampshire

Education Requirements for Licensure	Until January 1, 2005: B.A. Degree with accounting concentration. After January 1, 2005 and until June 30, 2014: 120 hours (including B.A. Degree or higher degree) with accounting concentration or equivalent. On or after July 1, 2014: 150 hours (including B.A. Degree or higher degree) with accounting concentration.
Hours Required in Accounting for Licensure	Prior to January 1, 2005: 12 semester hours in accounting. After January 1, 2005 and until June 30, 2014: 12 semester hours in accounting. On or after July 1, 2014: 30 semester hours of accounting courses. The accounting credits shall include coverage in financial accounting auditing, taxation, and management accounting.
Exam Sitting Requirements	B.A. (120 hours)
Accounting Experience Requirements for Licensure	Until June 30, 2014: B.A. Degree-2 years experience. Master's Degree in accounting, taxation, finance, or business administration-1 year experience. On or after July 1, 2014: 1 year experience. Can be gained through public accounting and governmental agencies.
Ethics Exam	No ethics exam

New Jersey

Education Requirements for Licensure	Complete all of the following: A baccalaureate degree from a regionally accredited institution, at least 150 semester hours of general college level credit, at least 24 semester hours in accounting courses, and at least 24 semester hours in general business courses
Hours Required in Accounting for Licensure	At least 24 semester hours
Exam Sitting Requirements	As of July 1, 2017, complete all of the following: A baccalaureate degree from a regionally accredited institution, at least 120 semester hours of general college level credit, at least 24 semester hours in accounting courses, and at least 24 semester hours in general business courses
Accounting Experience Requirements for Licensure	1 year of experience in the practice of public accounting or its equivalent, under the direction of a licensee, that includes evidence of intensive and diversified experience in auditing or accounting.
Ethics Exam	Complete a four-credit course on New Jersey Law and Ethics

New Mexico

Education Requirements for Licensure	150 hours (including B.A.)
Hours Required in Accounting for Licensure	30 semester hours or equivalent quarter hours in accounting, auditing and auditing related courses.
Exam Sitting Requirements	B.A. (120 hours)
Accounting Experience Requirements for Licensure	1 year experience in government, industry, academia or public practice.
Ethics Exam	Must pass AICPA Professional Ethics Exam for initial licensure

New York

Education Requirements for Licensure	150 hours (including B.A.). Alternatively, 15 years of experience acceptable to the State Board for Public Accountancy may be substituted for education for admission to the examination and licensure. This experience must be earned under the direct supervision of a U.S. certified public accountant (CPA) as outlined above in the Experience Requirements section.
Hours Required in Accounting for Licensure	33 semester hours in accounting with at least one course in each of the following areas: financial accounting and reporting; cost or managerial accounting; taxation; auditing and attestation services; fraud examination; internal controls and risk assessment; and accounting information systems. Also, 36 semester hours in general business electives in any combination of the following areas: business statistics; business law; computer science; economics; finance; management; marketing; operations management; organizational behavior; business strategy; quantitative methods; and information technology and systems.
Exam Sitting Requirements	B.A. (120 hours) including a course in each of the following: financial accounting and reporting; cost or management accounting, taxation; and auditing.
Accounting Experience Requirements for Licensure	1 year experience earned in a public accounting firm, government, private industry or an educational institution in one of the following service areas: accounting, attest, compilation, management advisory, financial advisory, taxation, or consulting skills. The experience must be gained under the

	supervision of a U.S. certified public accountant who is properly licensed and registered or authorized to practice in the jurisdiction of their principal place of business.
Ethics Exam	No ethics exam

North Carolina

Education Requirements for Licensure	150 hours (including B.A.) or should a candidate possess a Master's degree or more advanced degree in accounting, tax law, economics, finance, business administration or a law degree from an accredited college or university or the equivalent, the candidate is in compliance with the 150 hour requirement as defined by 21 NCAC 08A.0309 and the education requirement further noted in 21 NCAC 08F.0410 (a).
Hours Required in Accounting for Licensure	30 semester hours or equivalent quarter hours of undergraduate accounting (which includes no more than 6 hours of accounting principles) or 20 semester hours or equivalent quarter hours of graduate accounting courses open only to graduate students or a combination of undergraduate and graduate courses
Exam Sitting Requirements	B.A. (120 hours)
Accounting Experience Requirements for Licensure	The work experience requirement is one (1) year experience in the public practice of accountancy under the direct supervision of a properly licensed CPA; or one (1) year experience in the field of accountancy under the direct supervision of a properly licensed CPA; or four (4) years of experience in the field of accounting; or four (4) years of experience teaching accounting in an accredited college or university; or four (4) years of experience self-employed in accounting. If the applicant does not meet the one-year requirement, he or she must meet the four-year requirement.
Ethics Exam	Exam on North Carolina Rules of Professional Ethics and Conduct

North Dakota

Education Requirements for Licensure	150 hours (including B.A.)
Hours Required in Accounting for Licensure	24 semester hours or equivalent quarter hours in accounting courses (principles of accounting or equivalent courses do not count toward the required accounting)
Exam Sitting Requirements	Must be within six months of completing education requirement
Accounting Experience Requirements for Licensure	1 year of experience gained through employment in government, industry, academia or public accounting.
Ethics Exam	Must pass AICPA Professional Ethics Exam for initial licensure

Northern Mariana Islands

Education Requirements for Licensure	150 hours (BA Degree)
Hours Required in Accounting for Licensure	24 semester hours or equivalent quarter hours of upper or graduate level accounting and 24 semester hours or equivalent quarter hours of business at undergraduate or graduate level
Exam Sitting Requirements	150 hours (must complete education requirement before sitting for exam)
Accounting Experience Requirements for Licensure	2 years (2,000 hours) experience of public accounting in industry, government, academia or public practice
Ethics Exam	No ethics exam

Ohio

Education Requirements for Licensure	150 hours (including B.A.)
Hours Required in Accounting for Licensure	30 semester hours or equivalent quarter hours in accounting
Exam Sitting Requirements	150 hours (must complete education requirement prior to sitting for exam)
Accounting Experience Requirements for Licensure	1 year experience in public accounting: 150 hours or sat for the exam prior to 2000. 2 years public accounting experience: Sat for exam with less than 150 hours but obtained 150 hours prior to certification. The public accounting experience is gained through employment in government, business or academia.
Ethics Exam	Ohio Board of Accountancy course on basic professional standards and responsibilities

Oklahoma

Education Requirements for Licensure	150 hours (including B.A.)
Hours Required in Accounting for Licensure	30 semester hours or equivalent quarter hours in accounting courses above principles of accounting or introductory accounting (1 course is to be in auditing or assurance)
Exam Sitting Requirements	150 hours (must complete education requirement prior to sitting for exam)
Accounting Experience Requirements for Licensure	1 year public accounting experience gained through employment in government, industry, academia or public practice.
Ethics Exam	Must pass AICPA Professional Ethics Exam for initial licensure

Oregon

Education Requirements for Licensure	150 hours (including B.A.)
Hours Required in Accounting for Licensure	24 semester hours or equivalent quarter hours in accounting
Exam Sitting Requirements	150 hours (must complete education requirement prior to sitting for exam)
Accounting Experience Requirements for Licensure	12 months of full time employment in public practice, industry, government or other professional setting
Ethics Exam	Must pass AICPA Professional Ethics Exam for initial licensure or an exam on the Code of Professional Ethics offered by the Oregon Society of CPAs

Pennsylvania

Education Requirements for Licensure	150 hours (includes B.A. Degree). Note: In addition to the 24 hours required to sit for the exam, must have an additional twelve semester credits in accounting, auditing and tax subjects of a content satisfactory to the Pennsylvania board.
Hours Required in Accounting for Licensure	24 semester hours or equivalent quarter hours in accounting, auditing, business law, finance or tax subjects of a content satisfactory to the Pennsylvania Board.
Exam Sitting Requirements	B.A. (120 hours)
Accounting Experience Requirements for Licensure	1 year (1,600 hours) of experience in any type of service or advice involving the use of accounting, attest, compilation, management advisory, financial advisory, tax or consulting skills gained through employment in government, industry, academia or public practice acquired over a period of not less than 12 months.
Ethics Exam	No ethics exam

Puerto Rico

Education Requirements for Licensure	150 hours (BA Degree)
Hours Required in Accounting for Licensure	58 hours in the study of accountancy, business law, economics and finance, of which at least 32 hours must be in the study of accountancy
Exam Sitting Requirements	None
Accounting Experience Requirements for Licensure	Puerto Rico has two paths to licensure: 150 hours of education including a B.A. in accounting with no experience requirement; or graduate of college or university recognized by the Puerto Rico Board who has not completed required education but has practiced the profession for 8 years prior to the date of application
Ethics Exam	No ethics exam

Rhode Island

Education Requirements for Licensure	150 hours (including B.A.)
Hours Required in Accounting for Licensure	Graduate Degree with concentration in accounting. Graduate Degree accredited in business-24 semester or equivalent quarter hours in undergraduate accounting or 15 semester hours or equivalent quarter hours in graduate accounting or a combination thereof. B.A. Degree or higher degree 24 semester or equivalent quarter hours in undergraduate or graduate level accounting.
Exam Sitting Requirements	B.A. (120 hours)
Accounting Experience Requirements for Licensure	1 year experience gained through employment in public practice, government, industry, education or a combination thereof.
Ethics Exam	Must pass AICPA Professional Ethics Exam for initial licensure

South Carolina

Education Requirements for Licensure	**150 hours (including B.A.)**
Hours Required in Accounting for Licensure	36 semester hours in accounting courses that are applicable to a B.A., M.A. or Ph.D. and which cover financial accounting, managerial accounting, taxation and auditing of which at least 24 semester hours must be taught at the junior level or above. Additionally, 36 semester hours of business courses which may include macro and micro economics, finance, business law, management, computer science, marketing, and accounting hours not counted as part of the 36 hours in accounting.
Exam Sitting Requirements	120 semester hours (including B.A.). Must include at least 24 semester hours of accounting specific courses, including four mandatory courses to be taken at the junior level or above: auditing, intermediate/financial accounting, cost/managerial accounting, and a US tax course. There is a maximum of 12 semester hours of lower level courses accepted. Additionally, must have 24 semester hours of business courses. Credits earned through non-traditional methods are not accepted, (ie exempt by exam, placement credit, competency credits, credit for experiential learning, work/life experience, or prior learning assessment).
Accounting Experience Requirements for Licensure	1 year of accounting experience in public, governmental, or private employment under the direct supervision and review of a certified public accountant or public accountant licensed to practice accounting in some state or territory of the United States or the District of

	Columbia; or at least five years' experience teaching accounting in a college or university recognized by the board; or any combination of experience determined by the board to be substantially equivalent to the foregoing.
Ethics Exam	Must pass AICPA Professional Ethics Exam for initial licensure.

South Dakota

Education Requirements for Licensure	150 hours (including B.A.)
Hours Required in Accounting for Licensure	24 semester hours in accounting at the undergraduate or graduate level including elementary principles of accounting and at least one course in each of the following: intermediate or advanced accounting, auditing, taxation and cost accounting. Additionally, must have 24 hours in business courses other than accounting.
Exam Sitting Requirements	150 hours (including B.A.)
Accounting Experience Requirements for Licensure	1 year experience gained through employment in government, industry, academia or public practice providing any type of service or advice involving the use of accounting, attest, management advisory, financial advisory, tax, or consulting skills, all of which were verified by a licensee.
Ethics Exam	Must pass AICPA Professional Ethics Exam for initial licensure.

Tennessee

Education Requirements for Licensure	150 hours (including B.A.)
Hours Required in Accounting for Licensure	30 semester or equivalent quarter hours of accounting education including the elementary level. Not more than 3 semester hours may be internship programs which may be applied to the 30 hours in accounting. Candidates must have at least 24 semester hours of accounting courses at the upper division level, junior level courses or higher.
Exam Sitting Requirements	Must be within 200 days of completing education requirement
Accounting Experience Requirements for Licensure	1 year experience gained through employment in industry, government, academia or public practice. 2 years' experience for CPAs providing attest services
Ethics Exam	Must pass AICPA Professional Ethics Exam for initial licensure

Texas

Education Requirements for Licensure	150 hours (including B.A.)
Hours Required in Accounting for Licensure	30 semester hours of accounting courses (15 hours require physical attendance on campus and 2 credit hours must be in accounting or taxation research and analysis). Also required for licensure: 24 semester hours in upper-level related business courses (2 hours must be in accounting or business communications) and a 3-semester-hour board-approved ethics course.
Exam Sitting Requirements	150 hours (including B.A)
Accounting Experience Requirements for Licensure	1 year of full-time non-routine accounting work experience under the direct supervision of a licensed CPA. Non-routine accounting involves attest services, professional accounting services or professional accounting work and the use of independent judgment, applying entry level or higher professional accounting knowledge and skills to select, correct, organize, interpret, and present real-world data as accounting entries, reports, statements, and analyses extending over a diverse range of tax, accounting, assurance, and control situations.
Ethics Exam	Must pass exam on Texas Rules of Professional Conduct.

U.S. Virgin Islands

Education Requirements for Licensure	Until May 16, 2020: A baccalaureate degree or its equivalent, including at least 120 semester hours of education conferred by a college or university acceptable to the Board, with an accounting concentration or equivalent as determined by Board rule to be appropriate and one year of acceptable experience; or Graduation from a college or university recognized by the Board, but if the applicant has not completed the hours of study and subjects specified in Board's regulation, the applicant must have been engaged in the practice of public accounting or in the employ of a public accountant or certified public accountant, for three years preceding the date of application, or have been employed by the government of the Virgin Islands or by the federal government as an auditor, or as an internal revenue agent, or in a position of supervisory responsibility over auditors or internal revenue agents for at least three years preceding the date of application. Effective May 16, 2020: Completion of 150 semester hours of college education including a baccalaureate or higher degree conferred by a college or university acceptable to the Board with an accounting concentration or equivalent as determined by the Board.
Hours Required in Accounting for Licensure	Until May 16, 2020: Out of the 3 criteria options for the education requirement only one requires accounting hours: Degree from recognized college or university and complete 30 or more semester hours – requires 20 semester hours or equivalent quarterly hours in accounting.

Exam Sitting Requirements	None
Accounting Experience Requirements for Licensure	1 year of experience, certified by a licensee, and gained through employment in government, industry, academia or public practice.
Ethics Exam	No ethics exam, but there is a Local CPA Examination.

Utah

Education Requirements for Licensure	150 hours (including B.A.)
Hours Required in Accounting for Licensure	Graduate Degree: 24 semester hours or equivalent quarter hours in upper division accounting courses and 15 semester hours or equivalent quarter hours in graduate level accounting courses which must cover financial accounting, auditing, taxation and management accounting or combination of both. B.A. Degree: 30 semester hours or equivalent quarter hours which includes 16 hours in upper division accounting courses and 8 hours in graduate level accounting courses which must cover financial accounting, auditing, taxation and management accounting.
Exam Sitting Requirements	150 hours (must complete education requirement prior to sitting for exam)
Accounting Experience Requirements for Licensure	1 year experience applying accounting and auditing skills and principles that are taught as part of the professional education
Ethics Exam	Must pass AICPA Professional Ethics Exam for initial licensure

Vermont

Education Requirements for Licensure	Prior to 7/1/2014: B.A. Degree. On or After 7/1/2014: 150 hours (including B.A. Degree).
Hours Required in Accounting for Licensure	Prior to 7/1/2014: B.A. Degree plus 30 semester hours or equivalent quarter hours of accounting, auditing and related subjects. On and After 7/1/2014: 150 hours (including B.A. Degree) plus 42 semester hours or equivalent quarter hours of accounting, auditing and related subjects..
Exam Sitting Requirements	B.A. or completion of B.A. within 60 days
Accounting Experience Requirements for Licensure	Effective prior to 7/1/2014: 2 years experience: B.A. degree. The experience shall include public accounting experience and must include 500 hours of attest, of which no less than 200 hours must be related to the audit function. Effective on 7/1/2014: 1 year experience: 150 hours (B.A. degree). The experience shall include public accounting experience and must include 500 hours of attest, of which no less than 200 hours must be related to the audit function
Ethics Exam	Must complete a course of study in professional ethics for accountants acceptable to the Board

Virginia

Education Requirements for Licensure	150 hours (including B.A.)
Hours Required in Accounting for Licensure	24 semester hours including auditing, financial accounting, management accounting and taxation. Also required for licensure: 24 semester hours in business courses, with no more than 6 semester hours of accounting courses (not included in the 24 hours of accounting courses). Principles or introductory courses do not qualify in the 48 required hours.
Exam Sitting Requirements	120 semester hours (including B.A.) with accounting concentration or equivalent.
Accounting Experience Requirements for Licensure	Employed full-time equivalent of 1 year in academia, a firm, government or industry in any capacity involving the substantial use of accounting, financial, tax or other skills that are relevant. Whether other skills are relevant shall be determined by the Virginia Board of Accountancy on a case-by-case basis. Self-employment does not qualify as experience.
Ethics Exam	Must pass AICPA's Professional Ethics Comprehensive Course.

Washington

Education Requirements for Licensure	150 hours (including B.A. Degree)
Hours Required in Accounting for Licensure	24 semester hours in accounting subjects of which 15 are at the upper division or graduate level. Also required for licensure: 24 semester hours in business administration subjects at the undergraduate or graduate level.
Exam Sitting Requirements	150 hours (including B.A.)
Accounting Experience Requirements for Licensure	1 year general experience, verified by a licensed CPA, through the use of accounting, issuing reports on financial statements, management advisory, financial advisory, tax, tax advisory or consulting skills gained through the practice of public accounting and/or employment in industry, academia, or government.
Ethics Exam	Must pass AICPA Professional Ethics Exam for initial licensure.

West Virginia

Education Requirements for Licensure	150 hours (including B.A.)
Hours Required in Accounting for Licensure	30 semester hours of accounting (excluding Principles of Accounting), including a minimum of 6 credit hours in financial or intermediate accounting; 6 credit hours in auditing or accounting information systems (at least 3 must be in auditing); 6 credit hours in taxation; 3 credit hours in cost accounting, managerial accounting, governmental accounting or not-for-profit accounting; and 9 credit hours in accounting electives. Accounting internships or independent studies not exceeding 3 credit hours may satisfy this accounting elective requirement. *Also required for licensure: 3 hours in Business Law and 27 hours in Business.
Exam Sitting Requirements	B.A. (120 hours)
Accounting Experience Requirements for Licensure	1 year of experience, verified by a licensed CPA, providing any type of service or advice involving the use of accounting, attest, compilation, management advisory, financial advisory, tax or consulting skills. May be satisfied by employment in private practice, government, industry, not-for-profit organization, academia or public practice.
Ethics Exam	No ethics exam

Wisconsin

Education Requirements for Licensure	150 hours (including B.A.)
Hours Required in Accounting for Licensure	Graduate Degree: Concentration in Accounting. Graduate Degree from a business school: 24 semester hours or equivalent quarter hours in accounting at undergraduate level plus 15 hours in accounting at graduate level which includes financial accounting, auditing, taxation and management accounting. B.A. Degree: 14 semester hours in accounting or equivalent quarter hours in accounting at undergraduate or graduate level which includes financial accounting, auditing, taxation and management accounting.
Exam Sitting Requirements	Must be within 60 days of completing education requirement
Accounting Experience Requirements for Licensure	1 year experience of public accounting or its equivalent. Equivalent experience may be considered in government, industry, academia, law, self-employment (must be documented and presented in detail for Board consideration).
Ethics Exam	Must pass the Wisconsin online ethics exam

Wyoming

Education Requirements for Licensure	Prior to 1/1/2012: B.A. Degree or 150 hours (including B.A.) Effective 1/1/2012: 150 hours including a BA
Hours Required in Accounting for Licensure	B.A. Degree: 24 semester hours or equivalent quarter hours accounting courses which includes financial accounting, auditing, taxation and management accounting. Or 150 hours (including B.A. Degree): 24 semester hours or equivalent quarter hours in upper division or graduate accounting courses which includes business law, economics, management, marketing, finance, business communications, statistics, quantitative methods, technical writing, information systems or technology, ethics or other areas as may be determined by the Board.
Exam Sitting Requirements	Prior to 1/1/2012: 150 hours (must complete education requirement prior to sitting for exam) Effective 1/1/2012: 150 hours with BA degree must be completed and documentation that the requirement will be completed within 90 days of the application date.
Accounting Experience Requirements	Prior to 1/1/2012: B.A. degree - 4 years experience in public accounting. On or after 1/1/2010: 150 hours (B.A. degree) - 1 year experience in public accounting. Effective 1/1/2012: 1 year experience in public accounting. All public accounting experience shall be gained through employment in government, industry, academia or the practice of public accounting.
Ethics Exam	Must pass AICPA Professional Ethics Exam for initial licensure